Havana

CIGARS

To Sévan and his Grandfather

This edition published by
Barnes & Noble, Inc.
by arrangement with
Book Sales Inc.
114 Northfield Avenue
Edison, New Jersey 08837

1997 Barnes & Noble Books

This edition © 1997
© 1995 Copyright SARL
55-57, rue Brillat-Savarin F-75013 PARIS – FRANCE

M 10 9 8 7 6 5 4 3 2 1

ISBN: 0-7607-0519-4

Printed in Spain

Gérard Père et Fils

Havana

CIGARS

Photographs
Matthieu Prier

BARNES
&NOBLE
BOOKS
NEW YORK

Contents

Foreword

The Havana is more than a cigar, it is a world unto itself. A world of such richness that, as with all products catering to good taste and refined living, it requires some attention and culture to be fully appreciated.

This is why we decided to expand upon our previously published volume, *The Connoisseur's Guide to Havana Cigars*. Since this original guide dealt principally with the technical aspects of cigars, it seemed to us that the Havana deserved further homage – this time paid in particular to its incomparable aesthetic traits.

Our primary goal, therefore, was to give full attention to this aesthetic aspect of the Havana. As such, the chapters presenting the range of each brand of Havana offer the cigar enthusiast life-sized photographs of the cigars to study and admire.

Our second goal was to avoid technical jargon, making this volume as relevant and accessible to the neophyte as to the confirmed connoisseur. However, in our attempt to describe the evolution of a cigar's taste as it burns, we have had to resort to expressions such as "hay" for the first third of the cigar, "divine" for the second, and "slurry" for the last, as these are the metaphors currently used by Havanophiles.

Finally, let us emphasize that our evaluations concern only those cigars conserved with the utmost care, and especially those that have benefitted from optimal conditions of growth, maturation, and settling of quality.

And now, let us succumb to the inviting fragrances of our topic...

In Praise of Taste

One no longer says "smoke a cigar," but rather "savor a Havana." This expression represents more than a mere language nuance: it reflects the remarkable evolution of cigar connoisseurs in the last few years. Just as we have learned to pair food and wine by carefully matching the perfect vintage with a complementary meal, or perhaps with the mood of our guests – so should we treat the Havana. A Havana should be chosen as if in preparation for an honored ritual: it should be selected well in advance, with great consideration given to details such as the smoker's mood, the timeframe permitted, and the environment in which it will be enjoyed... In short, cigar smoking has become a true gourmet experience – that is, an experience of curiosity, education, and contentment.

Like all oral experiences, smoking a Havana appeals to all the senses. Sight, firstly, allows us to appreciate the cigar's amber hue as well as its quality and craftsmanship. Touch then evaluates the degrees of softness and smoothness that indicate the life of the cigar. Of course, the sense of smell comes into play by detecting woody, fruity, or spicy notes even before lighting, and fully savors these aromas during burning. Hearing also "savors" the cigar: the rustling of the embers that precedes the sound of the lighting. Finally, and most importantly, is taste – which when combined with a Havana produces a supremely pleasureable sensual encounter.

It seems that, in fact, the same gastronome who endeavored to better understand wines will inevitably venture into Havana territory, eventually discovering the innumerable riches of this world as well. Progressively, his tastes become more refined and diversified and he increasingly opts for aromas with more depth than before. Just as he once abandoned heavy wines, and those which were too tannic, he now expects from a Havana something more than power and warmth – more significantly, he makes selections based such subtleties as the time of day, the seasons, his own disposition... His palate has become a formidable instrument of appreciation that now allows him to taste the most delicate of nuances. He is simply no longer content with ordinary sensations lacking in complexity.

This is simply the story of the evolution of taste... Our grandmothers' cuisine has been forever replaced by a lighter, more refined gastronomy; similarly, today's Havana enthusiast appreciates other perfumes and other tastes than did yesterday's aficionado. Where he used to prefer powerful, sharp flavors that left a weighty imprint, he now tends to favor robustness, smoothness, comfort, and opts for blossoming, woody perfumes. The appeal of the experience resides within its very capriciousness and fragility, traits which are, in fact, reflections of the Havana itself. As with master winemakers, a great cigar is the product of joint efforts, of

Cigar smoking has become a true gourmet experience – that is, an experience of curiousity, education and contentment.

8

feverish anticipation, and of relentless toil. As an artisan, the cigar producer must constantly avoid the perils posed by the climate, the soil... by human error. There is no sure formula for a cigar; it rather comes to life as in a dream. And each one is a miracle, a renewed miracle, and yet one without a guarantee. Is it not thus that we appreciate all great things in life, that is, with emotion and respect?

Here you have the basic principles of this work. In focusing upon the role the cigar plays in the "art of living," *Havana Cigars* provides an excellent initiation into the magical world of the Havana. This journey of discovery begins with the general architecture of the cigar and the particulars of its body, then onto its aroma and taste, progressing through to its texture and colors – not to mention its extraordinary varieties. In remembering the great varieties of the past, and in paying homage to the master creators, an entire universe of diversity and adventure reveals itself to us... a world of beauty, balance and passion.

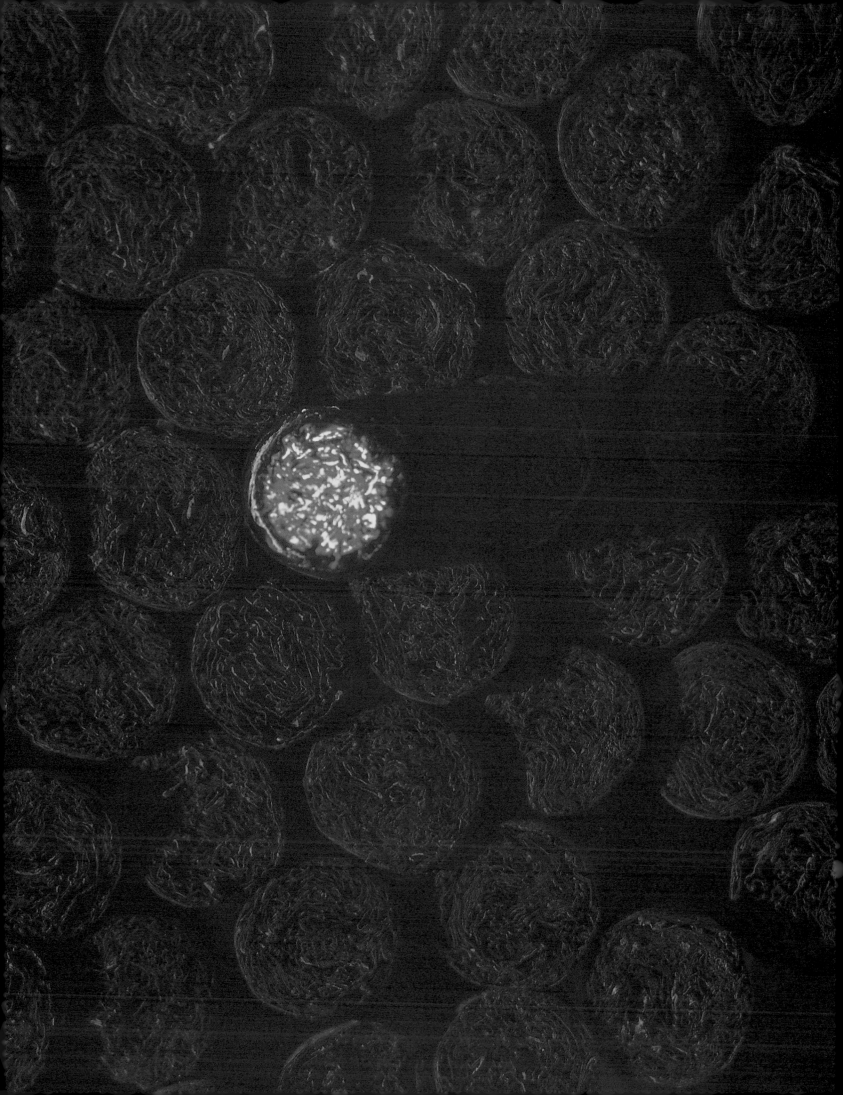

Bolivar

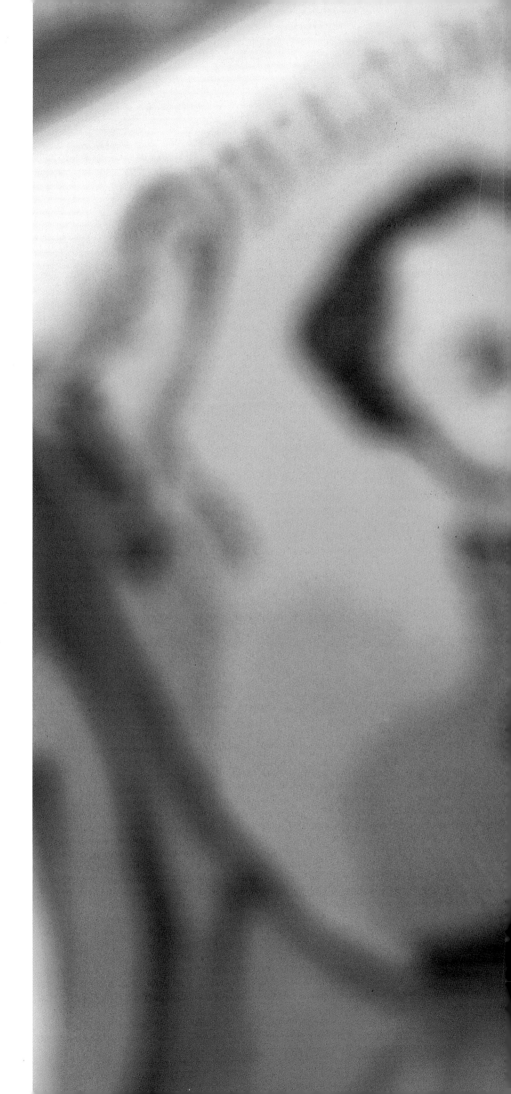

Bolivar does not carry the distinction it merits for its quality. Nonetheless, devotees of this brand are its most ardent defenders – and understandably so, as Bolivar has managed, over time, to intelligently compile an impressive assortment and a growing variety of aromas and tastes. As evidence, consider the smooth Royal Corona, perfectly adapted to modern-day preferences.

Bolivar's elaborate line, which includes many classics, today offers an astonishingly large range of flavors, from the very refined to the fullest-bodied. It does so despite the loyalty of its old fans who continue to prefer the traditional dry earthy aromas, enhanced by hints of spice, so characteristic of this cigar family.

We recommend: Coronas Gigantes in cabinet, Royal Corona, Petit Coronas, and Belicosos Finos for their elegance. Also, the Coronas Extra, for its richness.

ROYAL CORONA (robusto)
Unlike the rest of the Bolivar family, this generous robusto develops full, woody flavors without being aggressive. Its pronounced spices are seductive, while its relative subtlety caters to modern tastes.

PETIT CORONAS (petit corona)
With a rare straightforwardness, this petit corona makes an impression from the very first draw. Its rich, spicy, and woody traits emerge directly, almost instantaneously, and its responsiveness does not wane as it burns. A cigar for the connoisseur who likes a little excitement.

14

CORONAS GIGANTES (churchill)
This churchill distinguishes itself by its richness, substantialness, and by the complexity of its smooth flavors in a harmonious earthy-spicy range. The sweetness of the first draw opens onto more elaborate, powerful, and robust flavors.

ESPECIALES (gran panetela)
This extremely rare cigar boasts fine, intricate aromas and fresh, subtly sweet flavors enhanced by strong spices – all within a noble woody-vanilla range.

INMENSAS (lonsdale)
Here is a cigar for fans of the old Havana: very strong and very spicy, it is harsh, almost severely so, despite an easy, steady burn. A cigar of character, best reserved for educated connoisseurs.

LONSDALES (lonsdale)

This cigar is rather unique. Its very green perfume often gives the impression of immaturity – especially since it is followed up by earthy, somewhat matte flavors. It should be smoked in short draws as it has a very steady burn.

GOLD MEDAL (lonsdale)

Considered a collector's item, the very rare Gold Medal is distinguished by its breadth and aromatic richness. Its earthy and spicy qualities linger luxuriously in the air, ranking it in the echelon of Bolivar's great classics. Do not indulge in a Gold Medal, should the occasion arise, unless fully prepared.

BELICOSOS FINOS (figurado)

Although smoking one can be a bit unsettling, this little marvel is enormously appreciated by torpedo aficionados. The freshness of its first moments, which lasts up until its second third, is followed by a bouquet of rare complexity: one based on a mix of fruits and spices, invoking exotic bazaars. An excellent figurado.

CORONAS EXTRA (gran corona)

Above: in cabinet.
Opposite: boxed.
The most "Bolivar" of the Bolivars, the Coronas Extra is very strong, spicy, and earthy, yet, at the same time, consistent and refined. This gran corona requires a long maturation to reach its peak of quality. Its steady, slow burn accentuates its power, and it culminates in an explosive finale perfectly suited to ending rich meals featuring game or spicy ethnic dishes.

The Especiales

These are, as their name indicates, special cigars. Their length reaches between 9 1/4 and 9 7/16 inches (23.5 to 24 cm), and their diameter is traditionally about 3/4 of an inch (1.9 cm). These "kings" of Havanas are superb creations and really have nothing in common with each other aside from their rarity and their round shape. In fact, if other brands appear under two shapes – round and square – as long as they are presented in a case or in a box, these exceptional pieces, whose combustion can last beyond three hours, only lend themselves to a round shape, which seems to play a major role from both the point of view of taste – and its persistence – as well as of smoothness.

As for us – and this is a strictly personal opinion – we do not believe that the crowding of cigars one against the other in a box, nor the lack of oxygen this triggers, could deeply affect their taste; yet, it may affect the roundness of the cigars which would certainly be damaging for a product of this quality. Regardless of their respective tastes, the especiales' strongest point is their perfect shape which permits a discrete initial burn and a slow gradual release of aromas. Excessive compactness of the body of the cigar, therefore, is an obstacle that will inevitably impede drawing and diminish the sweetness of its perfumes. Yet, well-made and delightfully consistent, this cigar is perfect company at special occasions and celebrations.

From top to bottom:
Romeo y Julieta's Fabulosos
Sancho Panza's Sanchos
Punch's Diademas Extra
Montecristo A
Hoyo de Monterrey's Particulares

Cohiba

This great family of cigars is no longer known only because of its mythical name, Cohiba, which has been the subject of much debate since its creation in the late 1960s. Praised by some, critiqued by others, Cohiba, notwithstanding, enjoys considerable success – as is demonstrated by the exorbitant number of counterfeits it has generated.

This young brand has certainly succeeded in drawing a following, albeit one that remains divided over the plethora of choices it makes available. Nevertheless, Cohiba increased its line with the Linea 1492, comprised of the Siglo I, II, III, IV, and V. In fact, from their très petit corona, the Siglo I, to their churchill, the Esplendidos, Cohiba offers a remarkable variety of rich and elaborate tastes, mainly catering to the confirmed aficionado.

We recommend: the Esplendidos, with its aspect of a tenor; the Robustos, with its baritone accents; and the Siglo V, a veritable Havana diva.

ROBUSTOS (robusto)

With a complex blend of woody, clove, and winelike flavors, this is a smooth, easy cigar whose rich, comfortable, full-bodied flavors connect well with the palate. This little gem has only one weakness: it could be a bit longer. And yet, even this quality contributes to its charm, allowing for its enjoyment as a "companion" cigar.

CORONAS ESPECIALES (corona)

This delicious Havana boasting flowery, woody, and sweet aromas is characterized above all by its freshness. Easy to smoke, it would make an excellent cigar for the uninitiated smoker in search of complex flavor.

LANCEROS (gran panetela)

It may well have seen its hour of glory come and go; however, this elegant cigar, whose persistent floral perfume announces a grand, rich taste, still retains a loyal following. Admittedly, its density can be tiresome and may have somewhat diminished its charm. Nonetheless, the Lancero undoubtedly belongs to that category of grand cigars capable of marrying both elegance and taste.

CORONAS (corona)
The constancy of its aroma together with the fullness and complexity of its flavors won it brief access into the world of Cohiba. However, it was soon replaced by the Siglo III, whose flavor is even more in line with the character of the brand.

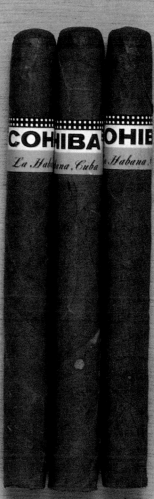

ESPLENDIDOS (churchill)
Considered the father of Cohiba, the Esplendido has rapidly gained a reputation among lovers of large cigars. Its rich, powerful taste and its spicy aroma place it among the most remarkable cigars of the churchill family. Its heavy, smooth aroma appeals mainly to educated connoisseurs. Steady burning, the Esplendido is an excellent evening cigar and complements fine dining marvelously.

EXQUISITOS (panetela)
This little cigar, full of ripe and robust flavors, is an easy smoke. It belongs to the category of quick-burning Havanas (they last about 20 minutes) specifically targeted to occasional smokers.

SIGLO V (lonsdale)

By virtue of its equilibrium, this beautiful, pure-bred cigar reminds one of the lonsdales in a Partagas cabinet. However, its rich, spicy flavor offers more acidity and less woodiness than its cousins. Its warm fragrances are evocative of damp earthiness. Most definitely a jewel among lonsdales.

SIGLO I (très petit corona)

This little cigar is a triumph of its genre: in tune with the times, it offers steady, quite rapid burning, and enlightens moments of relaxation as well as an aperitif. Its rich, slightly spicy aroma makes it a cigar with an instant taste that also appeals to women.

SIGLO II (petit corona)

The position of the Siglo II – one among many great Cohiba creations and one of a plethora of available petits coronas – is not an enviable one. It rises, however, to the challenge. Its oily and slightly spicy taste, maintained by woody notes, give it a distinctive quality and indisputably place it among great cigars of character.

SIGLO IV (gran corona)
Here we enter the realm of large cigars which is where the house of Cohiba truly excels. The Siglo IV possesses an amber perfume with nuances of musk, as well as a beautiful combination of somewhat peppery flavors that still allow for very sweet tones.

SIGLO III (corona)
Dignified successor of the coronas, this pronounced-tasting cigar is a perfect fit in the Siglo line and is very much a classical Havana – only without the headiness. Its longevity is not the least of its charms.

The Double Corona

These are – with the exception of the especiales –

the largest cigars available on the market with a length of at least 7 1/2

inches (19 cm) and a diameter of about 4/5 of an inch (2 cm). Since

their rise to popularity in the 1970s, they have been considered

"emperors" of the Havana and have become the object of a veritable

cult following. As with all elite ranges, the varieties of double coronas

have become increasingly limited, presently encompassing only the most

select products that adhere to the highest standards of craftsmanship.

Although it is not inconceivable that this restricted group

will one day expand – certain manufacturers, in fact, are already worthy

of its ranks – for now, only Partagas, Punch, Hoyo de Monterrey,

Saint Luis Rey and Ramon Allones include this size in their catalogues.

The double corona is a cigar of extraordinary fullness and

one whose first moments of somewhat cool subtlety give way quickly to

an exceptional livliness. Especially retained is the smoothness of the bou-

quet, where flowers blend with spices, offering deliciously

intoxicating sensations.

From top to bottom:
Punch's Double Coronas
Saint Luis Rey's Prominentes
Partagas' Lusitanias
Hoyo de Monterrey's Double Coronas
Ramon Allones' Gigantes

La Flor de Cano

A relative newcomer, La Flor de Cano gained its noble reputation during the 1980s by offering excellently crafted cigars made from the highest quality materials. In perfect harmony with its era, La Flor de Cano is distinguished by its sweet, uncomplicated tastes and has succeeded in seducing a large following of young day-time Havana smokers.

*T*his small, though exceedingly appealing selection has thus earned its place among our exclusive choices. Its only shortcoming rests in its very small production, which threatens to ultimately lead to its extinction. Needless to say, the world of the Havana would suffer considerably from such a disappearance.

DIADEMAS (churchill)
*This discrete cigar, with its sweet aroma
and appealing woody freshness, is easily
accessible and especially pleasant to
smoke on a summer afternoon.
It lacks just a little "something"
– perhaps power, intensity, or a
longer-lasting flavor – for inclusion
in the category of "great cigar."*

CORONAS (petit corona)
*The latest in the La Flor de Cano family, the Coronas is reminiscent of one's first
cigar. Sweet and steady, it is targeted in particular to novice cigar smokers, and,
indeed, many smokers have chosen it as their first foray into Havana territory.
Despite what its name might imply, the Coronas is actually a petit corona, whose
well-balanced line and beautiful roundness anticipate woody and fresh aromas. Its
simplicity has conquered many a palate.*

GRAN CORONA (gran corona)
*At once sweet and savory, this pleasant
cigar does not dominate by its power,
but rather by its suppleness.
Also noteworthy is its even burn,
which yields throughout an underlying
honeyed aroma, giving it an air of nobility.*

SHORT CHURCHILLS (robusto)
*This cigar makes its mark through its
grand, immediately perceptible generosity.
A little nourishing for some,
the Short Churchills tends to deliver all
its flavors during the first third. Its shape,
especially formulated for those preferring
full-bodied tastes, together with its mixed
aromas make it an excellent robusto that
is equally pleasing to neophytes.*

La Gloria Cubana

This brand is original in that it has maintained a standard selection of products within a range of very different formats – the Médaille d'Or N° 2 is testament to this fact. Indeed, while many brands have given over to medium formats, La Gloria Cubana has not modified its own.

Over the years, this family of cigars has attracted aficionados in search of pronounced yet unaggressive flavors. The brand also offers full aromas that are distinct from the spicy ones of the Partagas, with which La Gloria Cubana is, in fact, closely related.

We recommend: the Tainos and the Médaille d'Or N° 2, indisputably the thoroughbreds of the group; and the Médaille d'Or N° 1, a magnificent example of finesse and spirit.

TAINOS (churchill)
This authentic churchill, the heart of La Gloria Cubana, is a true original. Not only its taste, but also its presentation is distinctive: ten cigars in a flat box is a unique calling card. Although its rich, full flavor is less harsh than that of a N° 2, this cigar of elegant standing remains a magnificent after-dinner companion and an even and satisfying smoke.

MÉDAILLE D'OR Nº 1 (gran panetela)
This elegant cigar, slightly more discrete than its peers, further distinguishes itself by an excellent burn – a rare quality in this format – which yields spicy and woody scents. Its pronounced taste, a little aggressive in the last third, will seduce experienced connoisseurs seeking a satisfying nightcap.

MÉDAILLE D'OR Nº 4 (panetela)
Frequently compared to a corona, this cigar has a remarkably fresh aroma. A rather uncomplicated cigar, it yields seductive flowery and honeyed scents that often appeal to beginners. Well-built, it is an excellent daytime Havana, especially appropriate after a morning coffee or with aperitifs.

MÉDAILLE D'OR Nº 3 (panetela)

This elegant specimen is a pure-bred, aristocratic panetela. Contrary to expectations, its finesse and length do not hinder its burn, which is consistent from beginning to end. Its pervasive aroma develops in the initial two-thirds, and it ends with a powerful finale. Often recommended for women, the Médaille d'Or Nº 3 also appeals to fans of aperitif cigars.

MÉDAILLE D'OR Nº 2 (churchill)

Presented in a varnished box identical to that of 8-9-8 of Partagas, the Medaille d'Or 2 has a distinctive rich cocoa fragrance. Another trait in common with the Partagas cigar is its three-layer structure (8-9-8) which releases aromas as does the cabinet itself. The notes it yields in the palate are rich and creamy; the flavor is woody and lightly spicy. All this is released with perfection and beautiful evenness. Not at all aggressive, this churchill belongs to the grand tradition of the Havana.

The Churchill

Winston Churchill is definitely one of the great figures of the Havana; it is said that he could never be separated from his cigar. It is appropriate then that homage was paid to him by bestowing his name upon his favorite. This well-balanced size – traditionally at least 16 1/2 inches (17 cm) long with a diameter ranging from 11/16 to 12/16 of an inch (1.7 - 1.9 cm) – had been for the longest time the prerogative of a very limited number of brands. However, a range of remarkably differentiated churchills – with aromas from the sweetest to the most powerful – has gradually appeared on the market. Although this cigar, imposing by its size and diameter, is not to everyone's taste, its breadth of flavors makes it an ideal companion for the most diverse of meals – not to mention a great work companion. In fact, the churchill has a very special charm: comfortable to hold, with a very masculine line, it seduces from the very beginning, even before being smoked. A dozen manufacturers offer this size, with the best ones coming from Hoyo de Monterrey, Partagas, Punch and Romeo y Julieta – all very different types of churchills. All the same, the churchills of Bolivar, Cohiba, La Flor de Cano, La Gloria Cubana, Quai d'Orsay, El Rey del Mundo, Saint Luis Rey and Sancho Panza are certainly not to be overlooked.

left:
Bolivar's Coronas Gigantes
Saint Luis Rey's Churchills
Hoyo de Monterrey's Churchills
Cohiba's Esplendidos
H. Upmann's Sir Winston
Punch's Monarcas (aluminum tube)
La Flor de Cano's Diademas

right:
Sancho Panza's Coronas Gigantes
El Rey del Mundo's Tainos
Romeo y Julieta's Prince of Wales
Partagas' Churchills de Luxe
La Gloria Cubana's Tainos
Romeo y Julieta's Churchills
H. Upmann's Monarchs
Punch's Churchills

Hoyo de Monterrey

The history of this family could be summed up as a beautiful tobacco crossed with a lovely *fabrica* – a combination that yields marvelous cigars and whose secret recipe is jealously guarded by the craftsmen of this successful enterprise. The distinction of this brand lies in the sweet and aromatic flavors it offers. Sweet perfumes are combined with floral ambiances in a very complete, balanced selection of cigars that succeed in making a real impression on the palate without the use of overt spicy notes. Many aficionados started out with a Hoyo de Monterrey appreciating the "easiness," fresh taste, and consistent burn of, for example, the Epicure N° 2 or Short Corona, and then later graduated to the more pronounced traits of a cigar such as the Hoyo des Dieux.

The Hoyo series, which was born in the 1960s and has since drawn a loyal following, complements the offerings of this brand. Aside from the gran corona, Le Hoyo des Dieux, the line also includes a corona, Le Hoyo du Roi, a petit corona, Le Hoyo du Prince, a panetela, Le Hoyo du Gourmet, and a très petit corona, Le Hoyo du Député.

CHURCHILLS (churchill)

*Its smooth perfumes, both creamy and fresh, represent f
many the essence of its subtlety. A slow, yet full-bodied,
lution perfectly surrounds the palate, leaving a delicious,
mildly salty aftertaste. A grand master among churchills*

DOUBLE CORONAS (double corona)

*Considered among the sweetest of the type, this double
corona seduces by its enduring vanilla and honey perfumes. Complementary to grand meals, particularly to
refined nouvelle cuisine, this attractive Havana is further
enhanced by the quality of the meals and wines which pre-
cede it. Its regular burn allows for a constancy of sweetness in the palate and permits full enjoyment of its balanced flavors, which are consistent from start to finish.*

PARTICULARES (especiales)

*Of very fine taste and astonishingly discrete for its size, the
Particulares imposes itself as the most approachable of the especiales.
Its taste reveals itself in thirds and impresses to the smoker as much a
richness of aroma as it does a remarkable consistency. In a deceptive
manner (its matte perfume, a little dusty, lacks personality) this grand
format has a wonderfully fresh quality, making it a perfect choice for
pleasant summer evenings.*

EPICURE Nº 1 (gran corona)
*Rescued from anonymity in the 1980s,
this Epicure has slowly gained recogni-
tion thanks to its freshness and easiness. Also charming is its fruity and
honeyed bouquet. A wonderful daytime cigar, it is perfectly suited to
moments of reflection and meditation.
A word of warning: its perfectly regular
and generous burning may cause the
absent-minded smoker to forget to puff
on his cigar...*

SHORT CORONAS (petit corona)
*This little cigar of character is a per-
fect complement to the coronas. Its
easy access, between honey and flowers, brings out its woody notes.
Without spiciness, it distinguishes
itself through its roundness of aroma
and taste. In short, a wonderful part-
ner!*

EPICURE Nº 2 (robusto)
*This agreeable little cigar has offered
many neophytes the occasion to try their
first robusto. Its floral bouquet, brought
out by a touch of gingerbread, opens on
a completely unexpected, but pleasing,
fresh and dry note. A little short for an
after-lunch cigar, it is more suited to a
brief walk in the outdoors.*

LE HOYO DU ROI (corona)

This true corona with clean lines is a cigar of the shade. Homogeneous, it is more earthy than its other consorts in the line. Its spirited flavor, interrupted by a tinge of acidity, attracts old-fashioned enthusiasts, nostalgic for "the real Havana taste." Its constant burn makes it an excellent choice for an after-lunch cigar.

LE HOYO DU GOURMET (panetela)

A steady burn is not the least of the many qualities of this slender cigar whose sweet, somewhat faraway aromas become stronger once fully released. Not exactly an easy smoke, it can nevertheless be recommended to experienced Havana enthusiasts in search of a lighter daytime cigar.

LE HOYO DU DÉPUTÉ (très petit corona) (right)

This smart little cigar with a full-bodied taste can be enjoyed at any time of the day or night. It burns rapidly and emanates discrete, slightly honeyed aromas before fully revealing its liveliness to the palate, in a floral-acidic range.

LE HOYO DES DIEUX (gran corona)

While it is identified as a gran corona, Le Hoyo des Dieux is in fact an intermediary between this size and the lonsdale. A bridge in the range, it seduces by its richness and its depth of taste, which succeed in enhancing wonderful, flowery notes. A charming cigar that has earned an almost universal appreciation.

LE HOYO DU PRINCE (petit corona)

Slightly finer than the average petit corona, Le Hoyo du Prince is an excellent daytime cigar, equally appropriate in the morning, with an aperitif, or as a finale to a quick lunch. Its supple perfumes, just slightly acidic, are underlined by peppery flavors which do not overwhelm the palate. Its oxygenation, remarkable for its size, makes it one of the favorites of the series.

The Lonsdale

This attractively sized cigar – about 5 7/8 inches (15 cm) in length and with a diameter of about 5/8 to 11/16 of an inch (1.6-1.7 cm) – owes its name to the English aristocrat, Lord Lonsdale, who had a line of cigars of this format manufactured in his name. In fact, for many years, the house of Rafael Gonzalez, displayed a portrait of Lord Lonsdale on the inside of its boxes. Ironically, what is particular about these cigars, is that they don't possess any one particular quality with regard to taste.

They instead represent an extraordinary variety of aromas and flavors, from the lightest – that of El Rey del Mundo – to the most powerful. An example of the latter is offered by Partagas, a brand with the luxury to carry two cigars of this type: the Partagas N° 1 and the Lonsdale. The lonsdale format – which gained its reputation through the presently world-renown Montecristo N° 1 – is preferred by English-style enthusiasts who appreciate its elegance and discretion. Let us finally note that its presentation in cabinet is rare, and that most of the brands use the traditional box.

left:
Bolivar's Lonsdales
Bolivar's Gold Medal
Partagas' Lonsdales
Montecristo N° 1
Partagas de Partagas N° 1
Saint Luis Rey's Lonsdales

right:
Cohiba's Siglo V
Romeo y Julieta's Cedros de Luxe N° 1
Sancho Panza's Molinos
El Rey del Mundo's Lonsdales
Rafael Gonzalez' Lonsdales

H. Upmann

Although H. Upmann sometimes takes a back seat to other brands, we must note that, without this brand, an important chapter in Cuban cigar history would not have unfolded. Created by an English family during the last century, this cigar has long been the beacon of Cuban cigars, and, in fact, led to the appearance of the first Montecristo. One could not comprehensively discuss cigars without mention of some of H. Upmann's most beautiful creations – the nobility of which is reflected in the vignettes ornamenting its boxes.

Today's production of the brand is characterized by stronger, harsher and more earthy tastes than earlier versions; it is precisely this "distinguishedly rough" side of H. Upmann cigars that seduces its fans. Clearly, these are cigars destined for experienced smokers, and those loyal to the tradition of the Havana.

We recommend: two very different churchills: the majestic Sir Winston and the enterprising Monarchs; and the Connoisseur N° 1, an astonishingly light robusto.

CONNOISSEUR N° 1 (robusto)

This jovial robusto is a marginal H. Upmann. Easy to smoke, it possesses discrete aromas that are vaguely herblike, and a fresh, light taste. Its burn accentuates the charm of its simplicity. It belongs to the era of accessible cigars, appealing as much to the experienced smoker as to the beginner seeking an initiation to this format.

SIR WINSTON (churchill)

This beautiful cigar is the only churchill presented in a varnished box. Its full and rich aromas are due to its size which allows for their full release. Its excellent burn, which maintains a rhythm of constant flavor, is somewhat reminiscent of the double corona's. However, the most important trait of this fine, powerful cigar is its divine, simultaneously harsh and velvet quality. A superior churchill, round and well-built, that excels in accompanying rich meals and robust wines.

MAGNUM 46
(gran corona)

Since its distribution is limited, this gran corona with a fine and ample taste is practically unknown to the general public. This is regrettable since its rapid burning – about sixty minutes – is characterized by a veritable aromatic explosion between the second and last thirds.

CRYSTALES (corona)

This pleasant cigar is indisputably unforgettable – less because of the sweetness of its aromas and the suppleness of its discrete flowery-woody fragrances than because of its beautiful presentation. The Crystales of H. Upmann is, in fact, the last Havana still presented in a glass jar. Since the container is quite lovely, devotees of Crystales are most likely to be collectors in search of the cigar's precious – and generally empty – package in bric-a-brac shops.

UPMANN N° 2 (figurado)

With the exception of churchills, many H. Upmanns are comparable to the Montecristo. Yet, although these cigars are all products of the same factory, they still manage to maintain their distinctive qualities. Such is the case of this N° 2 torpedo. As powerful as one could desire, it blossoms fully in the last third and offers a satisfying finale. It is excellent after a heavy meal – an old-fashioned stew, for example – since it so perfectly embodies a return to rustic tastes.

MONARCHS (churchill)

Although its format is identical to that of the Sir Winston, it differentiates itself greatly by its piercing strength. Presented either alone or encased in an aluminum tube (for a richer and more aromatic taste) it appears very enterprising, yet lacks the personality of its glorious older sibling. Its promising style begs for an outdoor setting and cool temperatures – it would be ideal during a walk in the woods, after a satisfying lunch.

SUPER CORONAS
(gran corona)

This beautiful cigar is refined and aromatic, protected by a cedar leaf. Its sweet taste perfectly complements its ample burn which, over about sixty minutes, releases subtle and complex notes, ending with a very Havana-like finale. A word for enthusiasts of rare cigars: sold in very small quantities, the Super Coronas is extremely difficult to find.

Juan Lopez

*T*his old Havana manu-facturer offers only five hand-made cigars – always an indication of quality. Discrete, but well-established among Havana con-noisseurs, this brand geared itself to the trends of the 1980s, offering a gran corona and a robusto. This enabled Juan Lopez to recapture its former popularity by making its par-ticular taste known to a large number of cigar aficionados.

*M*ade from very sweet mixes, Juan Lopez cigars are light, pleasantly scented, and, therefore, accessible even to beginners.

SELECCIÓN Nº 1
(gran corona)

This beautiful cigar is very appealing to the new generation of Havana devotees who seek aromatic fragrances and a relatively light smoke. Its full and woody perfumes are typical of Juan Lopez. What distinguishes this cigar above all, however, is its very subtle palette of tastes – always within the same woody register – and its creamy feel. A rich and smooth cigar, it is very "colonial." A good choice for daytime smoking, whether after lunch or dinner.

CORONAS (corona)

Discrete and distinguished, this corona brings us back to the sources of Juan Lopez. Its beautiful leatherlike smell indeed evokes traditional tastes, with its spices unfolding in the last third. The sweet, even burn enhances the many qualities of this fresh seducer that never overwhelms the palate.

PANETELA SUPERBA (panetela)

The most recent addition to the Juan Lopez family, the Panetela Superba is a sweet cigar that neophytes may find appealing. Its slow burn produces small curls of smoke, making it very approachable.

PATRICIAS (très petit corona)
So easy that it is disconcerting, this très petit corona appeals above all to beginners. Its slightly green perfumes open onto a subtle flowery bouquet. Its charm resides primarily in the absence of arrogance once in the mouth — a quality which makes it a frequent companion to morning coffee.

SELECCIÓN Nº 2 (robusto)
Aficionados in search of a smooth, nonaggressive cigar will be very content with this delightful robusto from Juan Lopez. Exuding a multitude of exotic woody fragrances, it also offers a very aromatic, flowery bouquet. Extremely comfortable in one's mouth and without complexity, this cigar is a welcome ally during pleasant moments of the day.

PETIT CORONAS (petit corona)
This small, spirited cigar excels in the realms of charm, freshness, and lightness. Its beautiful, delicately fruity bouquet opens on sweet, simple notes that are appealing to beginners. Lacking tension, it burns well and is agreeable any time of day.

The Gran Corona

*M*asterpiece of the Havanas, the gran corona's

perfectly balanced length to diameter ratio (5/8 to 3/4 of an inch;

14-15 mm by 16-19 mm) has succeeded in attracting a following from

among half-robusto, half-corona enthusiasts.

Its success is especially due to the fact that it exists within an incredible

range of aromas and flavors – the house of Punch offering, from

this point of view, the richest of all, with a vast selection

from very sweet to very harsh.

In general, this size burns well, and its consistency makes it quite a

functional cigar. This guaranteed quality indisputably provides

satisfaction that a corona or a robusto cannot offer.

left:
Cohiba's Siglo IV
H. Upmann's Super Coronas
Partagas' 8-9-8 Cabinet Selection
Saint Luis Rey's Serie A
El Rey del Mundo's Gran Coronas

right:
Punch's Punch de Luxe
Rafael Gonzalez' Coronas Extra
Quai d'Orsay's Grand Coronas
Romeo y Julieta's Exhibición Nº 3
Bolivar's Coronas Extra

Montecristo

This great brand, which has long enjoyed an international reputation, saw the light of day in 1935 under the auspices of Mr. García and Mr. Menéndez – the latter being the owner of H. Upmann. It is said that in their early days Montecristos were not at all appreciated by cigar aficionados who preferred the more prestigious Upmann label. The following years, however, saw the qualities of the Montecristo validated, and the brand has since earned a first-rate reputation.

Montecristo is, in fact, one of the richest and most intelligent brands available: this quasi-mystical house undoubtedly owes its immense success to its remarkable opening and to the beautiful balance of its offering.

We recommend: the A, an ultra-masculine especial; and the N° 2, a harsh, very powerful torpedo.

MONTECRISTO Nº 5 (très petit corona)
*Very discrete in the floral range,
this moderate cigar is enjoyable
at any hour of the day.*

MONTECRISTO Nº 4 (petit corona)
*Challenging Nº 3 for the title of "best-selling
Havana in the world," Nº 4 has little
to envy in its brother.*

ESPECIALES Nº 2 (corona)
This smooth cigar has always been appreciated for its sweetness. Its elegant, discrete quality does not prevent it from revealing its woody, spicy self in the last third. Its smoothness remains a constant throughout the experience. Never corrosive, it is an easy and aromatic corona.

MONTECRISTO B (petit corona)
This superb petit corona, packaged in an old-fashioned box, is today considered a collector's item. Its woody, honeyed perfume, irresistibly evoking the islands, opens on a very aromatic, fresh, and light note, enhanced by an exotic nuance of caramel. An engaging cigar that does not lack in nobility.

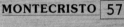

MONTECRISTO Nº 3 (corona)
This cigar's extraordinarily massive production is testament to its tremendous commercial success. Enough said.

MONTECRISTO Nº 1 (lonsdale)

The Montecristo Nº 1 has the draw of a classic. As such, devotees of reliable Havanas have long preferred it. With no trace of folly, it burns evenly and does not overwhelm the palate.

MONTECRISTO A (especial)

This emperor is incontestably one of the most beautiful accomplishments of Montecristo. Its rich and very present aromas are at first matte, then earthy, then increasingly concentrated, and, finally, become almost intoxicating in the last third. These open on a very tangy, expansive note that does not appear in the earlier stages, but becomes very pronounced later. A first-class repertory for this grand classic, whose power and smoothness appeal most of all to experienced connoisseurs.

ESPECIALES (gran panetela)

With regard to aesthetics, the Especial could easily win the title of "most elegant cigar." Even its shape – very slender with a twisted head – emphasizes its power and gives it a certain sense of excitement. Its pronounced taste and slow burn will seduce those Havana fans who are somewhat rough, yet worldly.

MONTECRISTO N° 2 *(figurado)

Where quality is concerned, the N° 2 is second to none. That is why, no doubt, both its detractors and its fervent supporters agree on classifying it among the great cigars of character. Its rich, powerful taste gives it incomparable style, as its powerful last third covers the palate with spicy and creamy aromas. Only for experienced connoisseurs.

The Corona

With an average length of 5 1/2 to 5 3/4 inches (14-15 cm) and

a diameter ranging from 5/8 to 6/8 of an inch (1.5-1.7 cm), the corona

is renown as the perfectly balanced cigar. This quality no doubt accounts

for the fact that it is the most widely available cigar format – and its

success is confirmed across brands, from the most discrete

to the most popular.

In fact, the corona is a very pleasant format; its excellent grip

and steady burn combine to make it an ideal daytime or after-meal

companion. Easy to handle, it provides sixty to seventy-five minutes

of even pleasure, with a very consistent progression throughout.

left:
Sancho Panza's Coronas
Juan Lopez's Coronas
Ramon Allones' 8-9-8 Cabinet Selection
H. Upmann's Crystales
Saint Luis Rey's Coronas
Romeo y Julieta's Cedros de Luxe Nº 2
Partagas' Coronas

right:
Romeo y Julieta' s Coronas
Ramon Allones' Coronas
Punch's Coronas
Montecristo Nº 3
Quai d'Orsay's Coronas
Cohiba's Siglo III

Partagas

This is one of the richest and most complete brands. Similar to Punch or Hoyo de Monterrey, it offers a vast range, from which we have highlighted only those that are most worthy of praise.

Partagas has built its reputation on two pillars: a large variety of choices – from the Très Petit Corona to the Double Corona – and a very distinctive highly pronounced taste. Its spicy, powerful fragrances are perceptible from the very beginning, and it maintains woody flavors that are sometimes sharp, sometimes creamy – on the whole offering the enthusiast an exceptional spectrum. The Partagas is always a perfect accomplice to hearty cuisines.

We recommend: for any time of day, the Connoisseur Series (Nos 1, 2, and 3); the 8-9-8 Cabinet Selection Varnished, a grand classic well-suited to rustic cuisine; the Lusitanias, best when paired with delicate meals and refined tastes; the Shorts, an excellent petit corona ideal for an aperitif; and the Lonsdales in cabinet, a marvelous complement to seafood.

**CHURCHILLS DE LUXE
(churchills)**
*This dynamo belongs in the ranks
of powerful cigars. A thoroughbred, almost harsh, it develops
spicy and earthy
aromas that give it a
rough edge, thus
appealing to smokers
seeking strength in a
cigar. Its earthy taste
complements game
entrees and strong spirits.*

**SÉRIE DU
CONNAISSEUR Nº 2
(corona)**
*Finer and longer than "real" coronas, the Nº 2
is a favorite of the new generation of followers, seduced by its panetela
allure. Very rich in flavor and aroma, it charms with its woody and lightly spicy, almost
fruity fragrances, which are savored fully with the help of a very easy burn.*

64

**PARTAGAS DE
PARTAGAS Nº 1
(lonsdale)**
*Of a classic shape, this tannic and dis-
tant Partagas has little in common, except
for its size, with the Lonsdale in cabinet. At
first very discrete, it takes awhile to impress
the palate, but, by the second third, its spicy
aromas manifest it as one of the last repre-
sentatives of the old-style Havana. A good
choice for experienced Havanophiles seeking
harsh tones.*

**SÉRIE
DU CONNAISSEUR
Nº 3 (petit corona)**
*This small Havana immediately makes its mark
through its subtle woody freshness, which is very pleasing to
young palates and fans of small, rounded curls of smoke. Undeniably
appealing, it makes an excellent initiation into the world of Partagas,
particularly for women who tend to appreciate its extraordinary elegance (at 14.2 cm of length). Especially suited to midmorning and
the aperitif hour.*

SHORTS (très petit corona)
In this breed, the Shorts have no equal. All vanilla and sugar, its generous curls leave spicy and salty peanutlike aromas on the palate. Definitely one of the best très petits coronas, it is well received by women and beginners who appreciate its freshness and smoothness.

SERIE D N° 4 (robusto)
This cigar is a deserving successor to its older sibling, the Serie D N° 2 – a gran corona with a churchill's diameter, today mostly forgotten. This robusto experienced its hour of glory in the 1980s, when this size was greatly in vogue. Admittedly, the N° 4 does have many merits: powerful and rapid, it yields a full-bodied aroma, with woody, spicy, very seductive notes. Rich and very present, it is astonishingly nourishing for this brand. A connoisseur's cigar.

SÉRIE DU CONNAISSEUR N° 1 (gran panetela)
Among the more recent creations of Partagas, the N° 1 lacks neither elegance nor strength. With an irreproachable appearance, it affirms itself in a rather harsh range and is penetrating with a very powerful finale. Rich and concentrated, it burns slowly, but very consistently. Nonetheless, approach with caution.

8-9-8 CABINET SELECTION
(gran corona)

The greatest disadvantage for this cigar has always been that it must live in the shadow of its glorious sibling, the Varnished. Nevertheless, once tasted and evaluated fairly and without bias, this gran corona proves entirely respectable. It burns well, and it will satisfy fans of discrete Havanas, as well as smokers who enjoy slightly spicy notes.

8-9-8 CABINET SELECTION VARNISHED
(churchill)

This cigar's famous presentation – three layers of 8, 9, and 8 pieces – leads to its rather unusual name. Its powerful aroma, with marvelous notes of cocoa, and rich taste are, however, the real sources of this heady churchill's reputation among connoisseurs.
Although some purists consider it a bit too fine for its format, even the most reticent have been overwhelmed by the fullness of its spices.
Very powerful, it only appeals to trained palates that can tolerate its harsh traits.

LUSITANIAS
(double corona)

Introducing the saint among saints of Havana. This superb cigar – one of the richest of the brand – captures one's attention with its magnificent bouquet of ripe fruit that opens onto amber flavors that, in their turn, evolve progressively toward spicier exotic notes. Its roundness and fruity flavor temper its strength and tannins; this cigar never tires the palate. An exceptional piece, with irresistible charm, aimed at connoisseurs.

PETIT CORONA (petit corona)

Discrete at first, but with a full-bodied taste, this petit corona with a bit of an edge appeals mainly to smokers who prefer harsh, not terribly subtle, cigars. This is the cigar for the outdoorsman who will appreciate its successive waves that border on aggressiveness. Exclusively for experienced Havanophiles.

CORONAS (corona)

A grand classic of both Partagas and coronas in general, this cigar has, in fact, built its reputation through its richness and nobility. A fine thoroughbred, it releases woody aromas with beautiful honeyed notes. Its mildly spicy taste has substantial charm. This pure corona's slow but very even burn offers plenitude.

LONSDALES (lonsdale)

Its race and ampleness make Partagas' Lonsdale a worthy competitor to the Punch Super Selection N° 1. The Lonsdales, with chocolate perfumes, is of the highest quality, and its longevity displays a harsh refinement. Very substantial and aromatic, it satisfies without tiring. Its unique, very noble style allows Partagas to demonstrate its abilities in areas in which it had not previously excelled: those of class and refinement. (The Lonsdales is difficult to find.)

The Robusto

*O*nly recently – in the 1980s and 1990s – has this type of cigar earned its

noble status, with its inclusion in the catalogues of brands such as Cohiba, Juan

Lopez, La Flor de Cano and Hoyo de Monterrey. Although the robusto was, in fact,

carried for many years by Partagas, Ramon Allones and El Rey del Mundo –

which were its true pillars – it was regarded with defiance due to its so-called

"lack of elegance" and the rustic quality of its full-bodied, yet little explored,

aromas. The present popularity of this stout, little cigar – it is at least 4 3/4 inches

(12 cm) long with a diameter of about 3/4 of an inch (2 cm) – is not surprising as

tastes evolve progressively toward more robust, powerful cigars, as well as toward

those with aromatic and spicy qualities. More significantly, perhaps, is that

the robusto accommodates modern smokers who no longer take hours to enjoy their

cigars, but, rather, look for quasi-instantaneous gratification in the experience.

In short, the robusto offers a satisfying epicurean equilibrium between

time of burning and richness of flavor.

It is only fair that this once disliked cigar – actually a great innovator of full-bodied,

direct flavors, and one that has provided a new perspective to many smokers –

should at last come into its own.

left:
Bolivar's Royal Corona
Romeo y Julieta's Exhibición N° 4
Saint Luis Rey's Regios
El Rey del Mundo's Choix Suprême

right:
Ramon Allones' Specially Selected
Cohiba's Robustos
Partagas' Serie D N° 4

Punch

P for princely, U for unique, N for noble, C for charming, H for Havana... the name of this brand of cigars is a veritable signature in anagram for its rare qualities.

*T*his great family is known for its high standards of production, as well as for the exceptional breadth of its selection which ranges from the especial to the petit corona. All boast strong aromas – mostly fruity or woody, depending on the type.

We recommend: the Double Coronas – Super Selection N° 1 and N° 2 – and the Royal Selection N° 12. All are jewels in the Punch diadem.

BLACK PRINCE
(gran corona)

With discretion and gentleness, the Black Prince reveals earthy notes through its delicate, peppery aromas. This combination gives it a very singular charm.
A seductive cigar.

ROYAL SELECTION Nº 11
(gran corona)

This savory cigar, among the most subtle of the gran coronas, derives its character from a very fresh first third and from the fruity and honey flavors, with slightly spicy undertones, that follow. Round and pleasing, its remarkable length-to-diameter balance lends it undeniable distinction.
A grand Punch classic, presented exclusively in cabinet.

ROYAL SELECTION Nº 12
(petit corona)

Without this little marvel, the universe of the petit corona would have been very different... Benefitting from perfect construction, the Royal Selection Nº 12 yields a great richness of woody aromas throughout an even burning. Both direct and smooth, it offers a creamy floral bouquet powdered with a fine peppery dust. It has continually improved over the last five years.

NINFAS
(panetela)

Elegant and well-constructed, the Ninfas is known for its constant burn that yields regular earthy and matte aromas. Somewhat monotonous, it nevertheless makes an excellent cigar for novices to this format.

DOUBLE CORONAS (double corona)

This beautiful cigar is one of the grand double coronas. Its woody, spicy, and earthy aromas open on very distinctive, never aggressive, tones in which honey accents a superb, powerful ascension of taste. The flavor is especially pronounced starting with the second third. This is definitely not a cigar for beginners, yet when its maturation and growth are at their peak, it is truly magnificent.

MONARCAS (churchill)

This imposing entity – the only Punch presented in a hand-made tube – is also the sweetest of the grand pieces of the brand. The discretion of its delicately spicy fragrances evokes the freshness of spring and yields a round, well-balanced, constant earthy and honeyed taste. All this is further enhanced by its slow burn. An excellent cigar for a summer evening. (This cigar is difficult to find.)

SUPER SELECTION N° 1 (lonsdale)

Halfway between a lonsdale and a gran corona, this superb cigar is a pure-bred, whose elaborate round tastes "melt" wonderfully in the palate. Spicy, woody, slightly honeyed and surprisingly balanced, its bouquet blossoms to the point of headiness – it is almost intoxicating. Only for experienced enthusiasts.

DIADEMAS EXTRA (especial)

Presented in individual boxes, this very appealing Havana possesses both nobility and elegance. This is undoubtedly why it reigns over the Punch family. The sweetness of its honeyed and woody aromas are constant throughout an ideal burning which leads to a magnificent crescendo, offering an extended period of intense pleasure. Not to be confused with the earlier generation of Diademas, created in a figurado format of 9 7/16 inches (24 cm), technically referred to as la diadema.

PUNCH-PUNCH DE LUXE
(gran corona)

An old friend of great aficionados, this homogeneous cigar has won a loyal following with its sweetness, making it the most popular of the gran corona Punch quartet – which also includes the Super Selection N° 2, the Black Prince, and the Royal Selection N° 11. Its round and flattering aromas open on a most savory honey-earthy melange. A true Punch classic.

CORONAS
(corona)

The corona format seems to be the great forgotten member of the Punch family. Certainly, Punch's selection is already quite rich, and its high-profile personalities numerous.... Actually, the Coronas, presented in a natural half-box and in cabinet, is satisfied with its average standing, without much subtlety. Taste it occasionally.

PETIT CORONAS (petit corona)

At one time, a cigar similar to this, called Ones, was available and was offered in an individual package. The Petit Coronas appears in a dry, earthy-honeyed range that is rather discrete, but not without charm. Never aggressive, it is an excellent cigar to take on a walk.

SUPER SELECTION N° 2 (gran corona)

Presented in a cabinet of 50 pieces, this gran corona is a perfect example of the best this brand has to offer. A complex bouquet, slowly evolving from woody flavors; earthy tones that are typically "Punch"; a rich, harsh, yet subtle flavor that clings divinely to the palate – these are the main qualities of the Super Selection No. 2. For experienced devotees on a quest for sensations...

CHURCHILLS (churchill)

This cigar is rather discrete for a churchill. But this lack of audacity is happily compensated for by a great richness of taste and an undeniable smoothness. Its matte and earthy aromas, slightly spicy, permeate the palate with sweetness and with a great precision, making it a veritable seducer.

PETIT PUNCH (très petit corona)

One of the best très petits coronas. With beautiful balance, the Petit Punch deploys a delicious honeyed, spicy bouquet, making it unique in this line. Its irreproachable burning enhances its aromatic richness, qualifying it as an excellent daytime cigar recommended for beginners.

Quai d'Orsay

This French brand was created in the 1970s by the Seita for French amateurs, and, over time, it has acquired a solid reputation.

Quai d'Orsay cigars are intended, above all, for experienced smokers who enjoy woody, slightly dry flavors, with, in the case of some its cigars, earthy tones. This brand's range does not rely on power, but, rather, on its aromatic richness.

We recommend: the Churchill Imperiales.

IMPERIALES (churchill)
*This very well-built churchill permeates
the palate with seductive woody notes.
Its aromatic character and lightness
emphasize its sweetness, which is
constant throughout a
slow and easy burn,
attractive to beginners.*

GRAN CORONAS
(gran corona)
*Pure and direct, this elegant cigar
– the finest the brand has to offer–
is distinguished by its matte, earthy
aromas, with a mild herbal quality
that builds toward woodiness. Its
beautiful balance and its easy
burning make it an ideal daytime
cigar – in fact, an excellent
companion for work.*

CORONAS (corona)
*Mythical in shape, pleasant in scent,
classical in aroma, aristocratic by name...
this corona has many attractive features. Its
dry and light qualities, enhanced by
acidic traits, become increasingly
forceful throughout burning and
evolve to a rather high range.*

The Petit Corona

*C*onsidered a small cigar – at about 5 inches

(12.5 cm), with a diameter of 5/8 to 3/4 of an inch

(1.6-1.7 cm) – the petit corona boasts a very large

production. It, in fact, represents a large portion

of all Havanas consumed, appealing to both daytime

and occasional cigar smokers. Two main reasons

account for this success: firstly, it has a relatively

short burning time – forty to fifty minutes -- which

makes it accessible, particularly after a light lunch.

Secondly, it possesses an agreeable distribution

of tastes throughout its structure, marked by lively

passages between the hay, the divine and the slurry:

a sequence of flavors that enhances the slightly edgy

character of the cigar.

left:
Rafael Gonzalez' Petit Coronas
Romeo y Julieta's Cedros de Luxe Nº 3
Bolivar's Petit Coronas

right:
Hoyo de Monterrey's Short Coronas
Cohiba's Siglo II
Ramon Allones' Petit Coronas
Sancho Panza's Non Plus
Montecristo Nº 4

Rafael Gonzalez

An established brand, Rafael Gonzalez is the perfect representative of the nobility of today's Havana cigars – though this brand undeniably knew a greater success in the days when green cigars (*clarísimos*) were the rage.

A distinguished classic, the present line is greatly appreciated by those who prefer rich and honeyed tastes with gingerbread aromas. Over the years this brand has developed a strong bond with its fans – a bond made up of seduction and fidelity. It is true that the class and discretion of this line afford it incomparable charm.

We recommend: the very elegant Lonsdale, for its "English Lord" allure; the Coronas Extra, for its kindness (a robusto-like burn in a gran corona body); and the Petit Lonsdales, for its charm, honey taste and gingerbread aroma that evoke spring, *joie de vivre* and pure freedom.

TRÈS PETIT LONSDALES (très petit corona)
Despite its small size, this très petit corona is unforgettable: smooth in the mouth, it develops rich and creamy flavors which differentiate it from the more powerful cigar. Ideal at the end of a traditional meal, it does not impose on the palate.

PETIT CORONAS (petit corona)
The most nervous of the Rafael Gonzalez family, it develops aromas that are green and has a woody flavor. Its last third, which is consumed at a very lively tempo, is perfectly suited for sampling at the end of a meal with sweet and sour flavors.

SLENDERELLAS (panetela)
Built with much finesse, this elegant panetela stands out because of its extreme sweetness and the freshness of its flowery note. Very rich tasting, it does not overwhelm the palate, which it leaves with hardly a trace. Well appreciated by amateurs of this line, it is an accessible cigar that holds a certain charm for both women and beginners.

HABANA

FLOR DE RAFAEL GONZALEZ
MARQUEZ
HABANA
HECHO EN CUBA

LONSDALES
(lonsdale)

Of a rare elegance, the Lonsdales is a magnificent cigar. Its slow burn offers the palate successive wafts of extraordinary perfume: honeyed and creamy aromas account for a large part of this seductor's charm, whose uncompromised quality of tobacco is also an important quality. One of the greats in this category.

CORONAS EXTRA (gran corona)

The largest format of Rafael Gonzalez, this is one of its best cigars. More powerful and rich on the palate than the Lonsdale, it is distinguished by a woody and slightly creamy taste which lasts throughout smoking. A comfortable cigar – not at all tiring – it is ideal after a good lunch or as company during reading.

PETIT LONSDALES
(petit corona)

Very aromatic and rich tasting, this petit corona is known for its amber perfume and its both woody and honeyed notes. A great marriage of power and smoothness that leaves the palate with delicious sensations. A rather original cigar for this line.

Ramon Allones

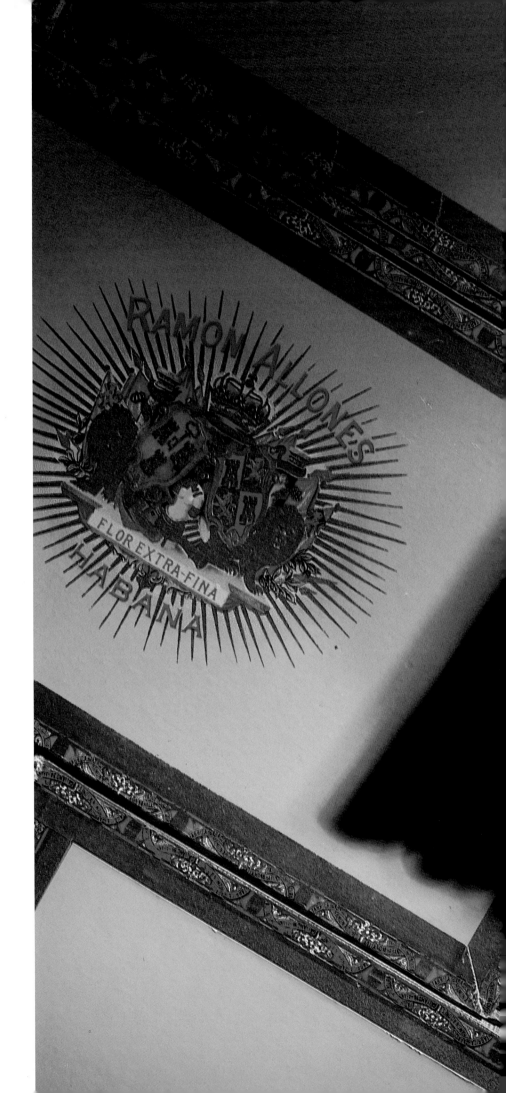

*C*ut from the same cloth as Partagas, this very old, internationally renown Cuban brand is characterized by strong, direct, frank tastes. Its vast range, which comprises all the classical sizes, is especially known for its double coronas, robustos, and coronas.

*P*rized by enthusiasts of cigars with body and essence, the Ramon Allones will forever grace grand tables and end holiday meals. These cigars, the products of exacting standards, are worthy of the great Havana tradition and appeal to serious amateurs. Collectors be advised: the Private Stock, a very chic lonsdale, is no longer produced.

We recommend: the Gigantes, a bewitching piece, very haute couture; the 8-9-8 Cabinet Selection Varnished, earthy and slightly spicy, equally haute couture; the Specially Selected, with the simplicity and fullness of beautiful ready-to-wear; and the Small Club, a mellow, very easy très petit corona which deliciously tantalizes the taste buds.

8-9-8 CABINET SELECTION VARNISHED (churchill)

Whereas, in the same cigar, Partagas offers an abundance of spices, the Ramon Allones version suggests delicious, honeyed, caramel perfumes. Ripe and creamy, it reveals great harmony in its smoothness. Long-lasting, its flavor develops within a sweet-salty range. Recommended for experienced smokers (though difficult to find).

8-9-8 CABINET SELECTION (corona)

Very different from the Varnished, this corona is discretion itself. Its sweetness suggests earthy, slightly matte tones. An easy daytime cigar, and one that is not aggressive on the palate.

GIGANTES (double corona)

Compared to other gran double coronas, the Gigantes is a powerful and generous cigar whose vitality sometimes borders on insolence. Its amber perfume immediately evokes an earthiness.
Its large body sticks to the hand like noble magic, enchanting connoisseurs. It is not a work companion – being too heavy, despite its subtlety – rather, it is a loyal friend at fine meals.

CORONAS (corona)

More understated than the rest of the Ramon Allones family (a quality that is its greatest strength) this corona, with earthy tones enhanced by a touch of spice, is neither tasteless, nor disappointing. A deserving classic, it appeals above all to aficionados of traditional Havanas lacking roundness. Especially appropriate at an autumn lunch.

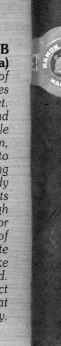

SPECIALLY SELECTED (robusto)

This, along with the Partagas and Cohibas, is one of three powerful choices of robusto. Full and ripe, it offers creamy tastes in the first third that later develop into stronger tones. Much fruit and aroma, as well as a touch of spice, confer upon it a lovely conviviality. Its comfort irresistibly evokes the feeling of well-being that one experiences in loosing oneself to the suppleness of old English leather worn by the passage of time.

PETIT CORONAS
(petit corona)

A small, slightly edgy specimen whose harsh taste – in the English style of earthy and slightly acidic tones – will seduce the fans of the old-fashioned Havana. Not as yet well-known, it nevertheless ranks among the most presentable cigars of the grand family of petits coronas.

SMALL CLUB
(très petit corona)

The amber of its perfume seduces from the very outset. The heavy and round aromas of this little cigar confirm its charm, as does its ability to maintain steady burning – thanks to its sturdy structure and its ventilation. Although perhaps too short for full development of flavor, it is still quite an enjoyable smoke from beginning to end. An engaging subject that can be enjoyed at any time of day.

The Très Petit Corona

This little cigar – 4 1/4 inches (11 cm) or shorter with a traditional

diameter of 5/8 of an inch (1.6 cm) – is very agreeable and does not

deserve the disdain that it has experienced up until now. A morning or

aperitif cigar, it allows for a pleasant smoke and ideally accompanies

Havana enthusiasts during their down time. We must not forget

to mention the favor this charmer has permanently captured

with the ladies thanks to its generous aromas. A final advantage:

the experience – which lasts between twenty and thirty minutes – is

characterized by a slight progression of aromas, since the très petit

corona does not offer up its entire flavor at once.

left:
Rafael Gonzalez' Très Petit Lonsdales
Romeo y Julieta's Très Petit Coronas
Partagas' Shorts
Montecristo N° 5
right:
Juan Lopez's Patricias
Sancho Panza's Bachilleras
Ramon Allones' Small Club
Romeo y Julieta's Petit Prince
Cohiba's Siglo I

El Rey del Mundo

The main characteristic of this regal brand is undoubtedly its sweetness which, whether dry or somewhat creamy, is found in all its formats. This trait, along with its freshness and lightness, makes El Rey del Mundo an excellent initiation to the Havana for a novice. Nonetheless, experienced connoisseurs of more powerful cigars are certainly not immune to the charms of this brand.

We recommend: the Tainos, a churchill; the Grandes de España, a gran panetela; and the Choix Suprême, a robusto.

LONSDALES (lonsdale)

This pleasant lonsdale comes in either in a natural wood box or in a natural half-box. Both formats are of equal quality – only the shape varies, whether round or square. As for flavor, this is an example of the grand tradition of El Rey del Mundo: light aromas, slightly dusty, in a woody-vegetal range. It burns well, enhancing the oral experience.

GRANDES DE ESPAÑA
(gran panetela)

The Grandes de España was created for those connoisseurs who appreciate elegance in terms of aesthetics as well as in quality and taste. This lovely panetela offers a pleasant vegetal perfume underlined by smooth traits and opens on discrete, pure, woody aromas. With a direct, somewhat marked flavor, it burns very well – so well so that its craftsmanship should be considered a work of art.

94

CHOIX SUPRÊME (robusto)

Very sweet for a robusto, the Choix Suprême develops creamy, honeyed, and green aromas simultaneously, making it a fine, easy-to-smoke companion cigar. As suitable in the morning as it is after lunch, it burns generously and is, therefore, very accessible. It is available in cabinet or in a natural half-box.

CORONAS (corona)

Clearly conceived for early morning smoking, this somewhat timid corona develops within a woody-vegetal range undeniably lacking in subtlety. Its matte qualities create an ephemeral taste in the mouth which would not satisfy a connoisseur – and yet might be pleasing to some at certain times of the day.

TAINOS (churchill)

Made from very fine leaves whose hues vary from a discrete golden matte to a well-nourished yellow, this churchill is among the freshest and lightest cigars one can find. Its dry aromas make it suitable for smoking throughout the day, and its easy and steady burning never tires. A good cigar for initiation to this size.

PANETELAS (panetela)

Here is, in brief, what this delicate panetela has to offer: a sweet and refined elegance, underlined by a savory, slightly sugary taste.

GRAN CORONAS (gran corona)

Available in a natural wood box and in a natural half-box, this gran corona is among the lightest on the market. Its excellent burning favors rapid smoking without tiring. Its range of flavor is classic "El Rey del Mundo": lightly herbal, slightly powerful, ending with an appealing bouquet.

Romeo
y Julieta

*I*m Laufe der Jahre hat sich dieses Haus einen ausgezeichneten Ruf bei den Liebhabern reichhaltiger und gut verarbeiteter Havannas gesichert. Die Marke wurde in der Tat bekannt, als sie leicht getrocknete Zigarren mit kräftigem Aroma, so recht nach dem englischen Geschmack, anbot. Sie hat es dann verstanden, nach und nach ein milderes, runderes und fruchtigeres Parfüm zu entwickeln, welches den Erfolg, namentlich der Fabulosos (eine Especial) oder der Exhibición No 4 in der Kabinettkiste (eine Robusto), bestimmt.

*M*an könnte die Entwicklung von Romeo y Julieta durch die zunehmende Beliebtheit ihrer drei großen «Stars» so zusammenfassen: in den 60er Jahren die Cazadores; in den 70ern die Churchills (reich, holzig, kräftig) und schließlich in den 90ern die Serie der Exhibición (sehr aromatisch, blumig). Romeo y Julieta ist unbestreitbar ein großes Haus, das sich zu erneuern verstanden hat und das den Erwartungen eines immer treueren Publikums stets gerecht wird.

E IN HABANA, CUBA

PETIT PRINCE (Très Petit Corona)

Dieser kleine «Kaugummi» unter den Havannas ist ein sympathisches Stück, dessen Frische und Leichtigkeit an die des Champagners erinnert – den es übrigens ausgezeichnet begleitet ... Einfach, ohne Komplikationen, kann sie zu jeder Tageszeit geraucht werden, ohne anderen Ehrgeiz, als die Muße einer kleinen Havanna-Pause zu bereiten ...

98

EXHIBICIÓN No 4 (Robusto)

Dieses Zigarrenwunder ist der perfekte Vertreter der neuen Havannageneration voller Anmut und Subtilität. Ihre Frische, ihre Ausgeglichenheit im Mund, ihr Zauber und ihre schmackhafte Tropenfrucht-Note wie ihr Gleichgewicht und ihr Komfort machen sie zu einem der Höhepunkte dieses Formats. Ein High-Society-Charmeur.

CAZADORES (Gran Corona)

Diese Gran Corona adligen Geschlechts ist ein Charakterkopf ... Ihr warmes Kakao-aroma führt in eine Welt, in der Reichtum und Geschmack an Übermut grenzen: Hier wird der Honig von betörenden Gewürzen abgedeckt und drängt zu einem herrischen Crescendo von außerordentlicher Kraft. Rassig und ohne Zugeständnisse, verdient dieses ungezähmte Raubtier zu Recht den Titel Cazador (spanisch für Jäger).

MADE IN HABANA, CUBA

EXHIBICIÓN No 3 (Gran Corona)
Zurückhaltender als ihre größere Schwester, die Robusto, bietet diese Gran Corona eine etwas schüchterne Annäherung. Doch ab dem zweiten Drittel entwickelt sie deutlich holziges und fettes Aroma. Dank eines sehr regelmäßigen Brandverhaltens hat sie eine schöne Länge im Mund.

CORONAS
(Corona)
Weder zu kräftig noch zu mild, verführt dies leichte, sehr angenehme Zigarre durch die Balance ihres waldigen Aromas. Ihre Frische gleicht die Cremigkeit ihres Geschmacks aus und ist so ein erlesener Begleiter von Einsteigern auf der Suche nach exotischen Nuancen.

TRÈS PETITS CORONAS
(Petit Corona)
Auf sympathische und einladende Art entwickelt sie ein köstliches Aroma von reifen Walnüssen, leitet dann über zu dichtem, säuerlichem und leicht erdigem Geschmack.

Romeo y Julieta 99

CELESTALES FINOS (Figurado)
Was bei dieser Figurado besonders beeindruckt, das ist ihre Fertigung nach alter Art: Bemerkenswert ist in der Tat das perfekt verjüngte Brandende. Aber nicht nur der Schnitt ist hier sehr traditionell, der Geschmack ist es auch, der sich in rustikal-kräftigen Noten darstellt und beim Erreichen des herrlichen Drittels eine seltene Kraft entwickelt. Auch wenn es nicht mehr in Mode ist, so bleibt dieses kraftvolle Kunstwerk doch eine ausgezeichnete Zigarre für Nostalgiker der traditionellen Havanna.

MADE IN HABANA, CUBA

CEDROS DE LUXE No 1 (Lonsdales)
Die Cedros No 1 ist zurückhaltend und eher leicht für eine Lonsdales und somit eine der am wenigsten akzentuierten Zigarren dieser Größe. Wegen ihres grün-würzigen Registers prägt ihr Aroma den Gaumen kaum, doch der frische und trockene Geschmack dürfte die Anfänger entzücken.

CHURCHILLS (Churchill)
Hier in der Tubus-Version dargestellt, gibt es sie auch ohne. Bei allen Havannafreunden bekannt, ist die Churchill von Romeo y Julieta wirklich das Paradepferd dieses Formates. Während sie durch ihre Präsentation in der Aluminiumhülse in die Geschichte einging, so hat sie sich bei den Liebhabern aufgrund ihres Geschmacksreichtums und ihrer Stärke einen Platz gesichert. Besonders kräftig ist sie im zweiten, sehr einschneidenden Drittel, dem sie ihren Ruf verdankt. Eine anspruchsvolle Zigarre für erfahrene Kenner. Auch ihre frischere Ausführung, ohne Tubus, wird sehr geschätzt.

PRINCE OF WALES (Churchill)
Sicherlich die mildeste im Churchill-Trio dieser Marke. Leicht und würzig am Anfang, wächst die diskrete Prince of Wales in einen betonten Holzcharakter hinein, der nur noch schwach würzig ist. Ihr entferntes Parfüm öffnet sich auf ein mattes, klassisches Aroma. Durch den sehr regelmäßigen Brandverlauf wird ein konstantes Geschmacksniveau gewährleistet.

CLEMENCEAUS (Churchill)

*Milder und leichter zugänglich
als die Churchill, prägen die
Clemenceaus trotzdem den
Gaumen mit ihrem holzig-
blumigen, durch würzige Noten
unterstrichenen Körper. Als
handwerkliches Produkt
erfordert sie eine gewissenhafte
Lagerung, um ihre volle Reife
zu erreichen. Sie ist der ideale
Begleiter zu traditioneller
Küche: zu Wildgerichten und
kräftigem Wein wirkt ihr erdig-
massiver Geschmack wahre
Wunder, noch unterstützt
durch ein gutes Brandverhal-
ten. Schwer zu finden.*

**CEDROS DE LUXE No 2
(Corona)**

*Die Cedros No 2 ist eine für dieses
Format außerordentlich leichte
Zigarre. Sie entwickelt sehr flüchtige
Kräuternoten über zurückhaltenden,
frischen und etwas holzgetönten
Aromen. Sie ist sehr mild und richtet
sich daher vorwiegend an Anfänger.*

**FABULOSOS
(Especial)**

*Mit ihren 24 cm, die
in feinste Deckblätter
gehüllt sind, ent-
wickelt dieser
Diamant unter den
Havannas Aromen
von seltener Subti-
lität. Es ist einleuch-
tend, daß ihr
prächtiges Maß eine
wichtige Rolle im
Reichtum ihres
differenzierten
Körpers spielt, wobei
ihr untadeliger
Brand zu einer
Konzentration der
Gewürztöne führt.
Kräftig, doch ohne
Aggressivität, verdient
es die Fabulosos, daß
man ihrer Reifung
eine anspruchsvolle
Sorgfalt zuteil werden
läßt.*

**CEDROS DE LUXE No 3
(Petit Corona)**

*Bekannter als die No 1 und die
No 2, besitzt die Cedros No 3 ebenfalls
außerordentliche Diskretion. Leicht,
etwas monoton, ist sie einfacher zugänglich
und kann ihren Platz als Begleitzigarre für
Liebhaber unkomplizierter Havannas finden.*

Gran Panetelas

Diese großen Verführer haben in den Jahren 1960–1970 einen beachtlichen Erfolg genossen. Sehr elegant – etwa 19 cm lang, mittlerer Durchmesser 1,5 cm –, erscheinen sie in der Tat als echte «Vollblüter», mit denen Kenner gerne anbändeln. Lange Zeit waren die Vorzeigeprodukte auf diesem Gebiet die Montecristo Especiales und die Davidoff No 1, dann – etwas feiner, jedoch ohne Panetelas zu sein – die Grandes de España von El Rey del Mundo und die Médaille d'Or No 1 von La Gloria Cubana, und schließlich kamen in den 80er Jahren die Lanceros von Cohiba auf den Markt. Diese Zigarren sind unbestreitbar alle Grandseigneurs – auch mit den dazugehörigen Launen. Denn die Architektur dieser Formate ist in Wirklichkeit sehr heikel: Für ein angenehmes Rauchen darf der Zug keine Schwierigkeiten machen, außer einem leichten Widerstreben, das das Ausbilden einer aromatischen Linie begünstigt. Dies ist bei einem solch eleganten Format keineswegs eine einfache Sache. Andernfalls geht der Punkt rasch auf das Konto der Mitstreiter. Das bedeutet anders gesagt, daß man wahrscheinlich mit den Gran Panetelas am besten die Entwicklung zwischen Kopf, Körper und Brandende während der 60 bis 90 Minuten des Brandverlaufs erleben kann. Abgesehen davon und im Gegensatz zu den meisten anderen Formaten sind sich die Zigarren dieses Formates überhaupt nicht ähnlich. Letzte Anmerkung: Die Gran Panetelas gibt es in zwei Kopfausführungen – leicht gezwirbelt oder abgerundet. Dieser Unterschied verändert den Geschmack in keiner Weise. Zum Schluß machen wir auf die (sehr vertraulich behandelte) Produktion der Trinidad aufmerksam, die den Ehrengästen der kubanischen Regierung vorbehalten ist.

Von oben nach unten:
Especiales von Bolívar,
Lanceros von Cohiba,
Médaille d'Or No 1 von La Gloria Cubana,
Grandes de España von El Rey del Mundo,
Especiales von Montecristo.

Saint Luis Rey

This historical brand, recently all but forgotten, reclaimed its place in the bosom of the grand Havana families in the 1980s. Its selection encompasses a rich and well-chosen spectrum of earthy and spicy aromas – mainly appealing to confirmed amateurs, but also offering a unique experience to the beginner.

The beacon of this selection is incontestably the Prominente – this double corona in a half-box is a little masterpiece. Indeed the entire court of this empire is more than respectable, with the serie A, a gran corona in the tradition of the franc tireur; the Regios, a robusto playing the role of court jester; and the Coronas, with the harmony of a minstrel.

PROMINENTE (double corona)
Difficult to find because of its very limited production, the Prominente is a nourishing, hearty Havana. Its access is easy thanks to its diameter, yet its initial curls soon cover the palate with aromas that evolve into earthy, heady tones. Powerful and very direct, this is a cigar for the experienced smoker.

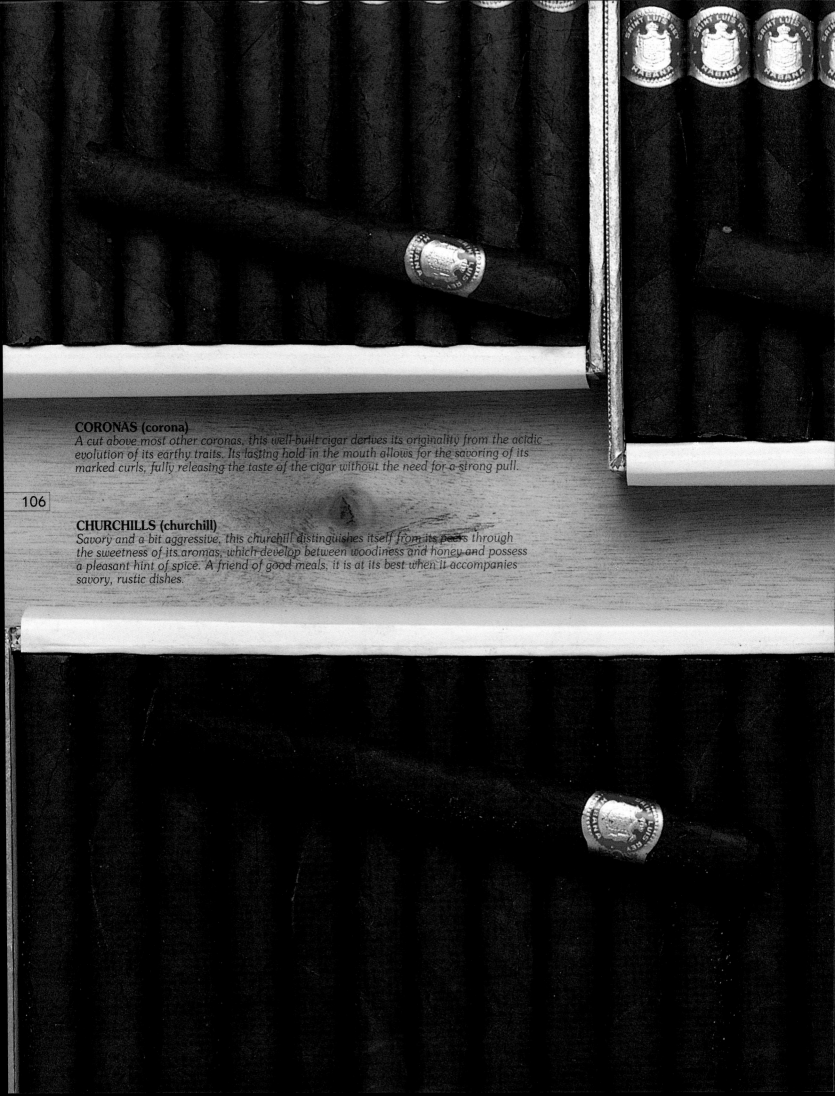

CORONAS (corona)

A cut above most other coronas, this well-built cigar derives its originality from the acidic evolution of its earthy traits. Its lasting hold in the mouth allows for the savoring of its marked curls, fully releasing the taste of the cigar without the need for a strong pull.

CHURCHILLS (churchill)

Savory and a bit aggressive, this churchill distinguishes itself from its peers through the sweetness of its aromas, which develop between woodiness and honey and possess a pleasant hint of spice. A friend of good meals, it is at its best when it accompanies savory, rustic dishes.

SERIE A (gran corona)
Round and well-balanced, the Serie A has a bewitching mix of animal and botanical fragrances – a summery musk – opening on full, progressive flavors. The evolution of aromas takes place within a woody spectrum, followed by a honeyed trace, before ending on a sustained note of warm exotic nuances. Undeniably seductive.

REGIOS (robusto)
A superb robusto, with a delicate chocolate and gingerbread fragrance. Long-lasting, it very subtly imposes its sweet and balmy aromas on the palate. Its steady burning accentuates its plenitude, making it a pleasant cigar whether accompanying a meal or a nightcap.

LONSDALES (lonsdale) (below)
Solemn – at least in appearance – this smooth Havana expresses its vitality through its rich, dry flavor. Its rustic fragrance unveils a hint of somewhat distant herbal and earthy scents, but it is an unusual mix of earthy-tart notes that give it its charm. Not for every palate.

The Figurados

This name covers a number of very different cigars, whose single common trait is a bottle-neck tip. (The Partagas' Presidentes even has a cone shape at both extremities.) Standing out from this heterogeneous group, is the torpedo – also referred to as the *piramide* – at 5 1/2 to 5 5/8 inches (14-15 cm) in length and with a diameter of 7/8 of an inch (2 cm). Montecristo, with its N° 2 cigar, has brought the most fame to this type, clearing the path for H. Upmann, Bolivar, and Sancho Panza whose cigars are no less appreciated even if they are somewhat shorter. Indeed, the torpedo has its fans, who fully appreciate its beautiful evolution of sensations – from the comfortable first moments, to the blossoming during the "great crossing," before the finale that is a veritable whirlwind of power and fullness. This format's flair lies in its unique construction: by merging at one end, it aromas are enhanced. This is why figurado amateurs are always fanatical about the taste of this cigar and continually seek out a wealth of perfumes and flavors – a trait which they share with aficionados of robustos and double coronas.

left:
Romeo y Julieta's Celestiales Finos (perfecto)
Bolivar's Belicosos Finos (torpedo)
Cohiba's Figurado (torpedo)
Upmann N° 2 (torpedo)

right:
Montecristo N° 2 (torpedo)
Sancho Panza's Belicosos (torpedo)
Partagas' Presidentes (perfecto)

Sancho Panza

*T*his very old Cuban brand, which still enjoys a great reputation among Havana fans, offers a well-balanced selection with, specifically, a churchill (Coronas Gigantes), a lonsdale (Molinos), and an especial (Belicosos). These three formats are accompanied by short cigars which round out the selection well.

*T*he success of Sancho Panza is undoubtedly due to the elegant and refined style of its sweet and aromatic blends, which cannot help but seduce a large following.

BELICOSOS (figurado)

Not to be judged by its appearance... Although torpedoes have a reputation as powerful cigars, this Belicosos develops in a sweet, light range – which, in fact, makes it a perfect initiation to this format. Very present in the palate, it is never aggressive, despite its full-bodied flavors, which allows for the full savoring of its charm.

112

CORONAS GIGANTES (churchill)

Its finesse, relative sweetness, and unique aroma make it a churchill that stands apart from the rest. With perfect harmony, the Coronas Gigantes has proven itself a refined accomplishment – one whose heady tastes and slightly intoxicating perfumes have conquered even the most subtle palates.

CORONAS (corona)

When Sancho Panza discussed the corona, it was undoubtedly in order to complete its line – and to come up with a cigar that was tune with the brand's style. Mission accompli Worth noting is its well-built consistency, which allows for a slow, pleasant smoke.

MOLINOS (lonsdale)

The Molinos is a gentleman. Its discrete, almost distant, perfumes place it, at first, below the level of respect it merits. But this aristocrat with a big heart soon delivers smooth, full aromas that are enhanced by a touch of caramel, before progressing, thanks to its excellent burn, into a beautiful tannic finale. A sweet and refined charmer.

...CHOS (especial)

...posing physique – at over 9 ... (23 cm) long – can be ...ding: neither harsh nor ...ssive, this giant operates in ...ness and lightness. The first ...possesses herbal and flowery ...s; the "divine" second third, ...h woody notes, faraway at ... of great refinement; and the ...ird manifests a gentle ...ning. Very present, the ...os is not ...ed for the ...iated – if ...ecause it ...three hours ...ke.

BACHILLERAS (très petit corona)

Of course, this très petit corona cannot compete with its older peers in terms of power and fullness. This, however, does not prevent it from being very engaging, with light flowery-sugar tones that make it enjoyable anytime. The right Havana for a coffee and croissant, it can be an especially pleasant start to the day.

SANCHO PANZA 113

NON PLUS (petit corona)

This petit corona first seduces by the presence of its woody notes, deprived of spicy elements. Without overpowering, it coats the palate beautifully, and it burns well thanks to the quality and construction of its components. The Non Plus belongs to the family of daytime cigars.

Cigarritos and Panetelas

Cigarritos are the smallest and most delicate hand-made

cigars with a length of 3 7/8 to 4 1/4 inches (10-11 cm) and

a diameter of 1/2 to 9/16 of an inch (1.2-1.3 cm). They are the delight

of those who do not have enough time to smoke a more important

breed since their burning takes hardly more than fifteen minutes –

and they are equally appreciated by women, who often

object to a larger format.

Panetelas measure from 3 7/8 to 6 2/3 inches (10-17 cm) with an

average diameter of about 1/2 an inch (1 cm). These are elegant cigars,

greatly appreciated by female Havana fans. However, they also attract

smokers of different sizes with their lightness which complements

an aperitif or coffee so well.

left:
Rafael Gonzalez' Panetelas
La Gloria Cubana's Médaille d'Or N° 4
La Gloria Cubana's Médaille d'Or N° 3
Rafael Gonzalez' Slenderellas
Rafael Gonzalez' Demi-tasse

right:
Cohiba's Exquisitos
Juan Lopez's Panetela Superba
Rafael Gonzalez' Cigarritos
Cohiba's Panetelas
El Rey del Mundo's Elegantes
El Rey del Mundo's Demi-tasse

Beyond Havanas

*N*ever has the cigar world experienced so much change as it does now at the dawn of the 21st century. One reason for this lies in the considerable efforts and accomplishments of tobacco-producing countries such as Jamaica, Honduras, and the Dominican Republic – countries that are contributing substantially to this evolution. In fact, they have significantly improved their products, in terms of both construction and quality of ingredients.

*Y*et we would not dare to compare the incomparable: we will refrain from judging a Honduran or Dominican cigar relative to a Cuban one, since even among Havanas there exist important differences. And, although the Havana continues to maintain its distinctiveness – as well as the favor of purists – it would be unfair to neglect to mention the other cigars that have certainly proven themselves worthy of praise.

Opposite:
Gérard Père et Fils'
Sélection des Sélections (made with
tobaccos of different origins)

Next page:
Dunhill Romanas and Samanas;
Arturo Fuente corona and double corona
(made in the Dominican Republic)

Glories
of the Past

They were the joy of many generations of Havana fans. Their reputations spread far beyond the borders of their country of origin, especially to North America and Europe. They had names such as Henry Clay (pages 122–123, 25 Diamantinos stored in their glass tubes); La Corona, bearing the same name as the factory that continues to produce them (pages 120–121, 25 Coronas); Maria Guerrero (pages 120–121, 25 Cedros de Luxe N° 2); Cabañas y Carbajal; Villar y Villar; and more recently, Don Candido, Don Alfredo and many others that have disappeared.

For obvious reasons, descriptions of their aromas are impossible to recreate here... let us simply state that these cigars were well adapted to the tastes of their respective eras. Nevertheless, the rare boxes in which they were once stored that have managed to survive are today valued with the same respect and consideration as authentic works of art.

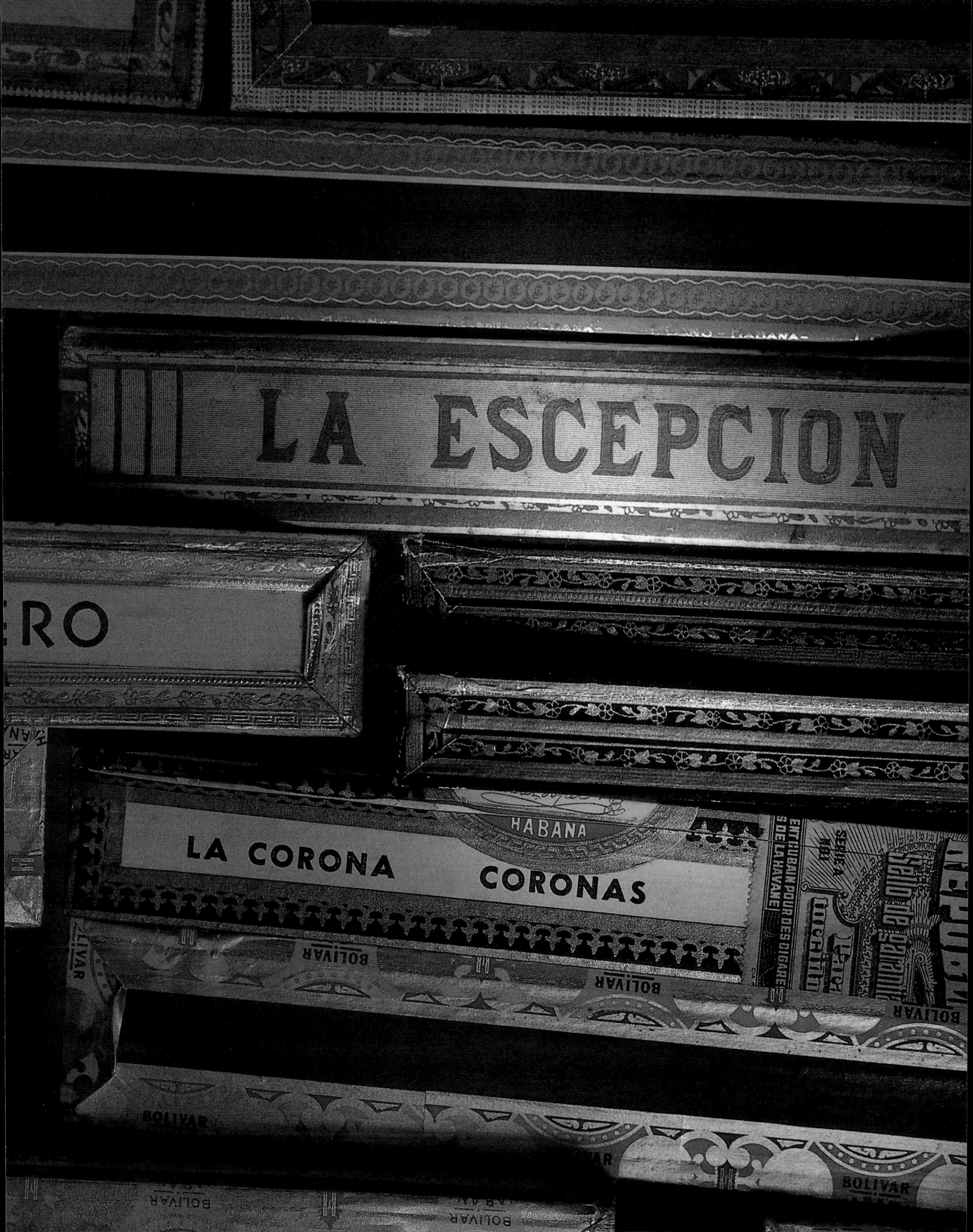
LA ESCEPCION
HABANA
LA CORONA
CORONAS
BOLIVAR

25 · MONARCHS · 25

Y JULIETA

Petit Prince

HECHO A MANO

LA ESCEPCIO

25 · CORONAS MAJOR · 25

Faded Heroes

*T*hey enjoyed their hour of glory until their reputations were eclipsed by that that of another rival... Nevertheless, one can still find them, albeit less and less often, usually behind some humidor, lonely in their oblivion, these cigars that once delighted many fans.

*T*he calling cards of these forgotten stars might read: Gispert (Petit Coronas de Luxe, opposite and on page 126); Por Larrañaga (Coronas, opposite and on page 126); José Gener La Escepción (Longos, pages 121 and 127); or even Diplomaticos (N° 1 and N° 6, opposite and on page 127) – this last house of cigars having survived only in the shadow of Montecristo, of which it has become a sub-brand.

A final mention goes to those whose unique format – a bundle of three braided cigars – qualifies it as a rare cigar called culebras (Partagas and Romeo y Julieta, opposite and on page 127).

The
Legends

*W*hile it is undeniable that the great brands are responsible for unveiling the beauty of the cigar to the entire world, it is no less true that this noble product is above all the result of the effort – and often hard work – of irreplaceable people who created, and continue to create, the world of the cigar.

*W*hether they toil in the heat of a plantation during harvest, or work in the secrecy of a factory concocting precious recipes, these artisans are entirely devoted to their product. Without these individuals, the history of cigars would be entirely different. Therefore, let us pay homage to grand masters such as Don Jaime Partagas, Alfred Dunhill, and Zino Davidoff, but also to those in the shadow of these legends who, each in his own way, contributed to and shared in their passion.

Next page:
Davidoff Aniversario
Dunhill Don Candido
Havana Club and Estupendo

ONE HAVANA CLUB CIGAR · MADE IN HAVANA CUBA

Rarest of the Rare

True, certain excellent cigars have completely vanished from the world; however, there do remain other extremely rare cigars that can be enjoyed... if, that is, one can uncover them!

They may be created in Havana for very special occasions (such as the torpedoes of Cohiba, on page 134, or the Clos Vougeot Figurados, presented in a little box, on page 137). They may be presented in old-style containers (such as the Montecristo B). Or they may be manufactured exclusively (such as the 25 Especiales Gérard Père et Fils Sélection des Sélections, page 140). Regardless, these marvels upon which time has bestowed a dreamy patina are the true joys of enthusiasts... and of collectors.

Opposite:
Partagas Palmas Reales Cristal Tubos

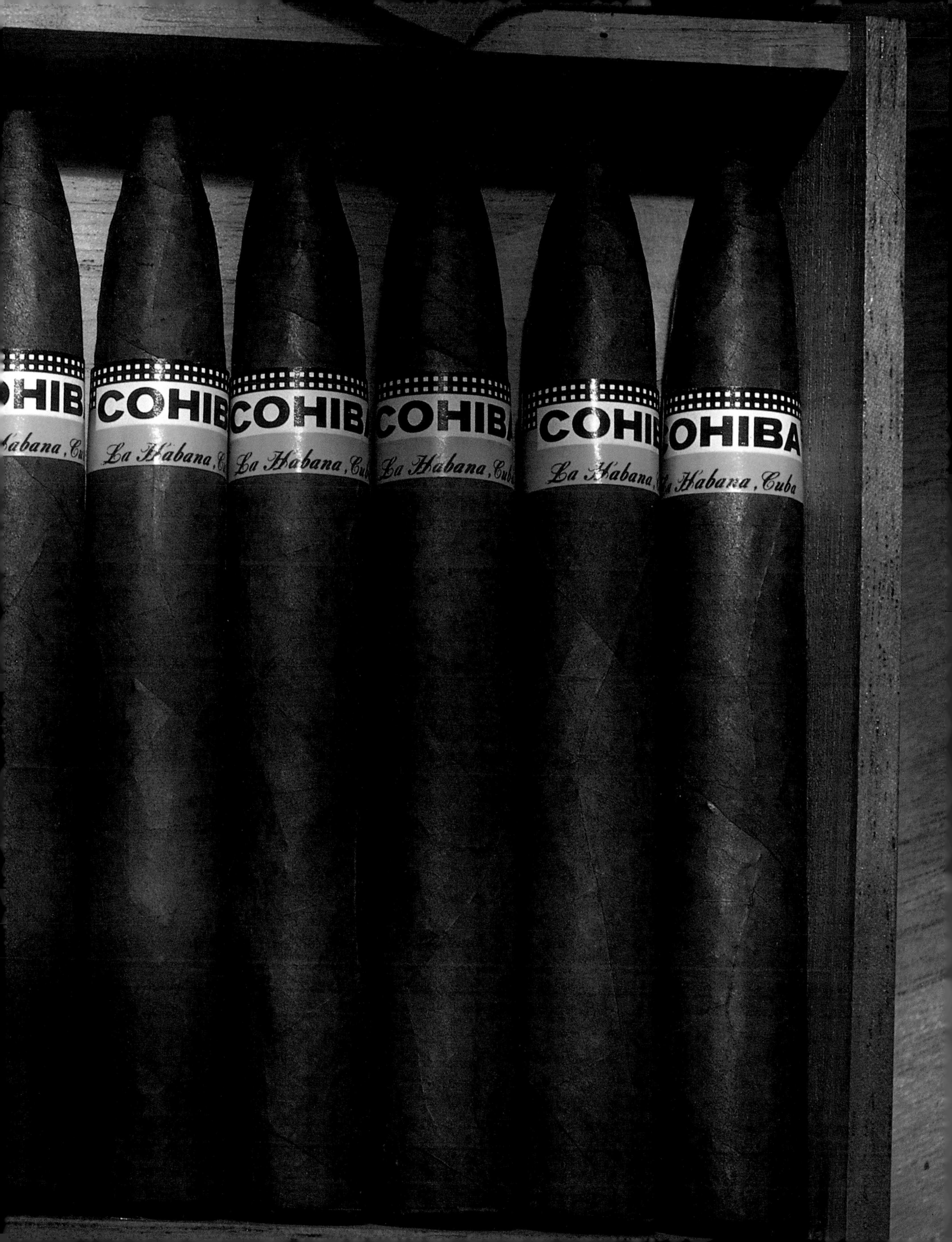
COHIBA
La Habana, Cuba

La Crème de la Crème

ssued in extremely limited series, these cigars are all beautiful collector's items, and their beauty, nobility and quality greatly enrich the cellars of connoisseurs. Some of them are considered actual art masterpieces and are fervently sought after.

iscovered one day in 1492 and brought to Europe by Christopher Columbus, this magnificent product, Havana tobacco, has become over five centuries the greatest friend of men in high places. Simply put, the Havana cigar is companion to all epicureans, happy to share in their pleasures of the palate or in the joy of a special moment, convivial and serene, and as for the delicious intoxication of each aroma, we could go on and on...

From top to bottom:
1492 (corona), created to commemorate the 500th anniversary of the discovery of Cuba; Gérard Père et Fils' Sélection (an old-style figurado) sold at Sotheby's in 1994; Clos Vougeot (figurado) presented in an individual box; Especial selected for the Parliament Club (1990); same size for the Nuit du Havane (Monte-Carlo); humidor of 50 gran coronas celebrating the 150th anniversary of the H. Upmann brand.

Epilogue

*L*ike all great journeys – especially those of discovery, enrichment, and blossoming – ours into the world of the Havana could be infinitely continued: there is definitely much material still to be covered. But let us try to be reasonable and find a way to close, with the grace of a final smoke curl, this volume...

*L*et us not forget to pay respectful tribute – with gratitude and affection – to all those before us who planted, cultivated, cared for, harvested, perfected, blended, manufactured, raised, in short, created these fabulous Havanas for our pleasure. Without the devotion, skill, and sometimes even courage, of the *vegueros* and *torcedores,* we cigar aficionados would simply not exist.

*N*or should we forget those who, for years, have made up the great family of Havanophiles – curious and attentive fans whose real talent inspires professionals to continuously improve

Opposite:
Gérard Père et Fils' Sélection des Sélections,
especial, in cabinet (discontinued series)
Next page:
Cigars from the private collection of
Gérard Père et Fils

and hone their craft. Their trust and valuable feedback are the surest ingredients of success, since, far from limiting themselves to arbitrary advice, the cigar maker's task is, above all, to understand the connoisseur, and furthermore to predict through them what the interests of future generations of Havana fans will be.

*F*inally, allow us to recall that a work such as this – a homage to the greatest of all cigars – would have never been possible without the full participation and constant devotion of our entire family. Our father, and all of us as well, have dreamt of conveying to you the essence of what he has taught us – that which today flows in our veins: the pursuit of supreme quality, the "sélection des sélections."

VAHÉ GÉRARD

Index

Noga Hilton - 19, quai du Mont-Blanc, 1201 Genève
Tel. 4122/732 65 11 - Fax 4122/738 64 73

All photographs in the book are by Matthieu Prier
apart from pages 6 & 7 and back cover (Daniel Boschung)

Produced by Copyright Paris